P9-CFF-764

PRESIDENTS

HARRY S TRUMAN

A MyReportLinks.com Book

Judy Alter

MyReportLinks.com Books

an imprint of

Enslow Publishers, Inc.
Box 398, 40 Industrial Road
Berkeley Heights, NJ 07922
USA

MyReportLinks.com Books, an imprint of Enslow Publishers, Inc.

Library of Congress Cataloging-in-Publication Data

Alter, Judy, 1938–
   Harry S Truman: A MyReportLinks.com Book / Judy Alter.
     p. cm. — (Presidents)
   Includes bibliographical references (p.) and index.
   Summary: Traces the life of the president who ordered the dropping of nuclear bombs
on Japan. Includes Internet links to Web sites, source documents, and photographs
related to Harry Truman.
  ISBN 0-7660-5069-6
   1. Truman, Harry S, 1884–1972—Juvenile literature. 2. Presidents—United
States—Biography—Juvenile literature. [1. Truman, Harry S., 1884–1972. 2. Presidents.]
I. Title. II. Series.

E814 .A48 2002
973.918'092—dc2l
[B]

                           2001004268

Printed in the United States of America

10 9 8 7 6 5 4 3 2 1

To Our Readers: We have done our best to make sure all Internet addresses in this book
were active and appropriate when we went to press. However, the author and the Publisher
have no control over, and assume no liability for, the material available on those Internet
sites or on other Web sites they may link to. The Publisher will try to keep the Report Links
that back up this book up to date on our Web site for three years from the book's
first publication date. Any comments or suggestions can be sent by e-mail to
comments@myreportlinks.com or to the address on the back cover.

Photo Credits: © Corel Corporation, pp. 1 (background), 3; Courtesy of
America's Story from America's Library, p. 30; Courtesy of Experience Kansas
City, p. 44; Courtesy of Harry S. Truman Library, pp. 16, 17, 25; Courtesy of Ibis
Communications, Inc. presents Eyewitness, p. 26; Courtesy of Project
Whistlestop, pp. 18, 20, 28, 31, 33, 40, 42; Courtesy of The National Atomic
Museum, p. 12; Courtesy of Truman Presidential Library & Museum, pp. 23, 34,
37; Library of Congress, p. 1; National Archives, pp. 14, 38.

Cover Photos: © Corel Corporation (background); White House photo courtesy
of the Harry S. Truman Library.

Contents

MyReportLinks.com Books
Great Books, Great Links, Great for Research!

MyReportLinks.com Books present the information you need to learn about your report subject. In addition, they show you where to go on the Internet for more information. The pre-evaluated Report Links, listed on **www.myreportlinks.com**, save hours of research time and link to dozens—even hundreds—of Web sites, source documents, and photos related to your report topic.

To Our Readers:

Each Report Link has been reviewed by our editors, who will work hard to keep only active and appropriate Internet addresses in our books and up to date on our Web site. However, the author and the Publisher have no control over, and assume no liability for, the material available on those Internet sites, or on other Web sites they may link to.

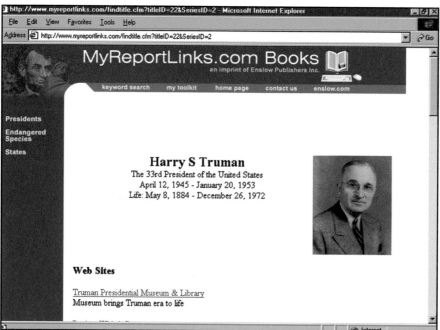

Access:

The Publisher will try to keep the Report Links that back up this book up to date on our Web site for three years from the book's first publication date. Please enter **PTR1843** if asked for a password.

Report Links

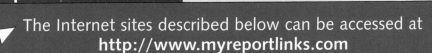

The Internet sites described below can be accessed at
http://www.myreportlinks.com

*EDITOR'S CHOICE

▶ Truman Presidential Museum & Library
This site offers a wealth of resources that bring the era of
Harry Truman to life. Some features include detailed chronologies,
oral histories, and online exhibits.

Link to this Internet site from http://www.myreportlinks.com
*EDITOR'S CHOICE

▶ Project WhistleStop
This site is a treasure-trove of Truman documents and memorabilia.
Here you will find official documents, personal letters, photographs,
and much more.

Link to this Internet site from http://www.myreportlinks.com
*EDITOR'S CHOICE

▶ Harry S Truman
Examine facts and figures on Harry S Truman. You will also find links
to Truman's election results, cabinet members, historical documents,
and other resources.

Link to this Internet site from http://www.myreportlinks.com
*EDITOR'S CHOICE

▶ Character Above All: Harry S Truman
In this excerpt from an essay by David McCullough, Truman's
character is explored from the time he arrived in Washington as a
senator, to the Election of 1948.

Link to this Internet site from http://www.myreportlinks.com
*EDITOR'S CHOICE

▶ Harry S Truman: A 50th Anniversary Commemoration of His Presidency
Biographer Robert H. Ferrell remembers Harry S Truman on the
fiftieth anniversary of his presidency. Ferrell provides a biography of
Truman, which covers his life and administration.

Link to this Internet site from http://www.myreportlinks.com
*EDITOR'S CHOICE

▶ The American Presidency: Harry S Truman
At this site you will find the inaugural address of Harry S Truman,
quick facts, and a detailed biography of his life and presidency.

Link to this Internet site from http://www.myreportlinks.com

Report Links

 The Internet sites described below can be accessed at
http://www.myreportlinks.com

▶**American Presidents: Life Portraits: Harry S Truman**
This profile of Harry S Truman provides facts and figures on Truman's life.
This is an ideal resource for quick reference about Truman and his presidency.

Link to this Internet site from http://www.myreportlinks.com

▶**Architects of Victory: Six Heroes of the Cold War**
This chapter, from Joe Shattan's book, *Architects of Victory: Six Heroes of the Cold War*, discusses Truman's foreign policy toward Soviet expansion.

Link to this Internet site from http://www.myreportlinks.com

▶**The Avalon Project at the Yale Law School: The Papers of Harry S Truman**
This collection of Harry Truman's papers chronicles the key events of his presidency. These papers include Truman's inaugural address, the Truman Doctrine, presidential proclamations, and executive orders.

Link to this Internet site from http://www.myreportlinks.com

▶**The Cold War Museum**
The Cold War Museum covers the Cold War from its beginning to its end.
Take a virtual tour where you can view images and art work of the times.

Link to this Internet site from http://www.myreportlinks.com

▶**The Decision That Launched the *Enola Gay***
This essay provides insight to the behind the scenes discussions that led to the decision to drop the atomic bomb on Hiroshima. Interestingly enough, Truman did not even know of the bomb's existence until he became president.

Link to this Internet site from http://www.myreportlinks.com

▶**For European Recovery: The Fiftieth Anniversary of the Marshall Plan**
Here you will find a complete history of the Marshall Plan. This site provides numerous links to speeches and descriptions of its various stages.

Link to this Internet site from http://www.myreportlinks.com

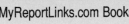
Report Links

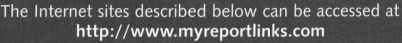

The Internet sites described below can be accessed at
http://www.myreportlinks.com

▶ **Harry S Truman**
This site contains an analysis of Harry S Truman's administration,
as well as a biography covering his early life and rise in the
political arena.

Link to this Internet site from http://www.myreportlinks.com

▶ **Harry Truman (1884–1972)**
The National Portrait Gallery holds a painting of Harry S Truman,
painted by Greta Kempton, Truman's favorite artist.

Link to this Internet site from http://www.myreportlinks.com

▶ **Harry S Truman, Diary, July 25, 1945**
This site contains an excerpt from Truman's diary where he discusses
his decision to drop the atomic bomb.

Link to this Internet site from http://www.myreportlinks.com

▶ **Harry S Truman: Inaugural Address**
Bartleby.com's vast electronic library holds the inaugural address of
Harry S Truman, delivered on January 20, 1949.

Link to this Internet site from http://www.myreportlinks.com

▶ **Harry S Truman: Kansas City's Fascination with the
Legacy Continues**
Although he was born in Lamar, Missouri, Truman considered
Independence his home. This site explores Truman's ties to
Independence and Kansas City.

Link to this Internet site from http://www.myreportlinks.com

▶ **Man of the Year**
For the past seventy years, *Time* magazine has recognized a person,
good or bad, for the impact they have had on the world. In 1949,
Harry S Truman received the Man of the Year award. At this site,
you can read the article written about Truman.

Link to this Internet site from http://www.myreportlinks.com

Report Links

▶**Mutual Admiration and a few Jokes**
This article explores Harry S Truman's relationship with the Marx Brothers.
Learn how they continued to correspond with each other over the years.

Link to this Internet site from http://www.myreportlinks.com

▶**The National Atomic Museum: The Decision to Drop**
At this site you can take a virtual tour and learn the history of the atomic age.

Link to this Internet site from http://www.myreportlinks.com

▶**Objects from the Presidency**
By navigating through this site you will find objects related to all the
United States presidents, including Harry S Truman. You can also read
a brief description of Truman, the era he lived in, and learn about the
office of the presidency.

Link to this Internet site from http://www.myreportlinks.com

▶**President Harry S Truman**
This profile reviews the highlights of Truman's presidency. Here you will find
an interesting fact about Truman, a quote, and a brief biography.

Link to this Internet site from http://www.myreportlinks.com

▶**The Presidents: Truman**
This site focuses on the life and political career of Harry S Truman. The
profile provides a detailed examination of Truman's presidency and legacy.

Link to this Internet site from http://www.myreportlinks.com

▶**Thoughts of a President, 1945**
Here you will read about the day Harry S Truman received the news
of Franklin Delano Roosevelt's death. You will also find an entry from
Truman's diary.

Link to this Internet site from http://www.myreportlinks.com

Report Links

 The Internet sites described below can be accessed at
http://www.myreportlinks.com

▶**Truman Announced A Fair Deal**
Here you will learn about Harry S Truman's "Fair Deal" program.

Link to this Internet site from http://www.myreportlinks.com

▶**Truman—Cold War**
At this site you will learn about Truman and the Cold War. Read the
text of Winston Churchill's "Iron Curtain Speech" and Joseph Stalin's
response to Churchill's speech. You will also find links to Truman
documents, NATO, and the Korean War.

Link to this Internet site from http://www.myreportlinks.com

▶**Truman, Harry S**
DiscoverySchool.com provides a profile of Harry S Truman. Here you
will learn about Truman's early life, political career, first and second
administrations, and retirement.

Link to this Internet site from http://www.myreportlinks.com

▶**The White House: Elizabeth Virginia Wallace**
Shortly after Harry Truman moved with his family to Independence,
Missouri, he met Bess Wallace, a classmate of his, and decided she
would one day be his wife. This profile of Bess Truman is part of the
White House History series.

Link to this Internet site from http://www.myreportlinks.com

▶**The White House: Harry Truman**
The official White House Web site holds the biography of Harry S
Truman. Learn about some of the crucial decisions Truman made
as president.

Link to this Internet site from http://www.myreportlinks.com

▶**1948: Harry S Truman (D) vs. Thomas E. Dewey (R)**
The *New York Times* learning network provides a summary of the
Truman vs. Dewey election. Here you can read a *New York Times*
excerpt on the outcome of the 1948 election.

Link to this Internet site from http://www.myreportlinks.com

Highlights

1884—*May 8:* Truman is born in Lamar, Missouri.

1890—Family moves to Independence, Missouri.

1901—Graduates from Independence High School with classmate Elizabeth (Bess) Wallace.

1905–1911—Serves in Battery B of Missouri National Guard.

1917—Rejoins National Guard. Sworn into regular army service in August.

1918—Fights in France during World War I.

1919—Marries Bess Wallace in Independence, Missouri.

1922—Wins election as eastern judge on the Jackson County Court.

1924—*Feb. 17:* Daughter, Mary Margaret, is born.

1927—Is sworn in as presiding judge of the Jackson County Court.

1934—Elected to the U.S. Senate.

1941—Truman Committee is created to investigate National Defense Program.

1944—*Nov. 7:* Elected vice president of the United States.

1945—*April 12:* Sworn in as thirty-third president of the United States.

—*July 17–Aug. 2:* Attends conference at Potsdam, Germany.

—*Aug. 6:* Announces dropping of first atomic bomb on Hiroshima, Japan.

1946—*Dec. 31:* Signs proclamation declaring the end of hostilities of World War II.

1947—*March 12:* Announces Truman Doctrine, requesting aid to fight spread of Communism.

1948—*June 26:* Orders Berlin airlift.

—*Nov. 2:* Elected to second term as president.

1949—*Aug. 24:* Announces signing of North Atlantic Treaty, creating the North Atlantic Treaty Organization (NATO) for the defense of Western Europe.

1950—*June 26:* Orders air and sea forces to aid South Korea.

—*Oct. 15:* Meets with General Douglas MacArthur on Wake Island.

—*Dec. 6:* Writes angry letter to music critic Paul Hume.

1951—*April 11:* Removes MacArthur as commander of United States and United Nations forces in the Far East.

1952—*March 29:* Announces decision not to run for re-election.

1953–1955—Works on his memoirs.

1956—*April 21:* Attends marriage of his daughter, Margaret.

1957—*July 6:* Harry S. Truman Library dedicated in Independence.

1972—*Dec. 26:* Dies at the age of eighty-eight.

The Atomic Bomb, August 1945

President Harry S Truman first met Premier Joseph Stalin and Prime Minister Winston Churchill at the Potsdam Conference held in Potsdam, Germany, in 1945. Churchill and Stalin knew the late President Franklin D. Roosevelt. They were uncertain about the new president. The purpose of this meeting of the Big Three—the United States, Great Britain, and the Soviet Union—was to discuss the future of Germany after its defeat in World War II, the continuing war with Japan, and the future of Western Europe.

At Potsdam, Truman received a strangely worded telegram: "Doctor has just returned most enthusiastic and confident that the little boy is as husky as his big brother."[1] The message meant that the first atomic bomb (Big Brother) had been successfully exploded at Alamagordo Air Base in New Mexico. The second bomb, Little Boy, was ready to be used against Japan.

Truman had to make a major decision. Army Air Force General Hap Arnold argued for bombing Japan with conventional weapons until the country surrendered. A single B-29 raid on Tokyo had wiped out sixteen square miles of the city and killed 78,650 people.[2] But it could still take weeks, months, or even a year before Japan might surrender. Truman believed the Japanese would fight to the death as they had vowed.

The Potsdam Declaration, signed by the Big Three, called on the Japanese to surrender or face utter destruction. The Japanese refused. Truman gave orders for the atomic

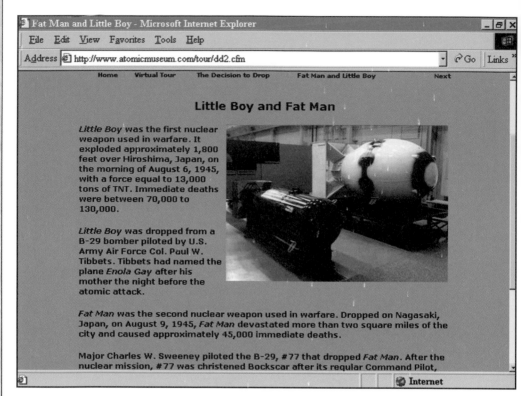

Home   Virtual Tour   The Decision to Drop   Fat Man and Little Boy   Next

Little Boy and Fat Man

Little Boy was the first nuclear weapon used in warfare. It exploded approximately 1,800 feet over Hiroshima, Japan, on the morning of August 6, 1945, with a force equal to 13,000 tons of TNT. Immediate deaths were between 70,000 to 130,000.

Little Boy was dropped from a B-29 bomber piloted by U.S. Army Air Force Col. Paul W. Tibbets. Tibbets had named the plane *Enola Gay* after his mother the night before the atomic attack.

Fat Man was the second nuclear weapon used in warfare. Dropped on Nagasaki, Japan, on August 9, 1945, *Fat Man* devastated more than two square miles of the city and caused approximately 45,000 immediate deaths.

Major Charles W. Sweeney piloted the B-29, #77 that dropped *Fat Man*. After the nuclear mission, #77 was christened Bockscar after its regular Command Pilot,

Internet

▲ *Little Boy and Fat Man were the first nuclear weapons used in warfare. The* Enola Gay *dropped Little Boy on the city of Hiroshima, Japan, on the morning of August 6, 1945. Another B-29 dropped Fat Man on Nagasaki, Japan, just three days later. The two nuclear devices devastated the cities.*

bomb to be used. The first nuclear bomb used in war was dropped on August 5, 1945, from the aircraft *Enola Gay* onto the city of Hiroshima, Japan.

President Truman issued a statement demanding that Japan surrender. Leaflets were dropped over the Japanese countryside, urging the people to stop the war. They also warned people to leave the big industrial centers to save themselves. Still, Japan did not surrender. A second bomb was dropped on Nagasaki on August 9. Emperor Hirohito of Japan finally surrendered on August 14.

A Controversial Act

Estimates are that two hundred thousand people died as a result of the Hiroshima bomb. Not all died immediately. Many suffered from radiation exposure, which caused a variety of problems. These included genetic defects, such as the birth of malformed babies and sterility, or the inability to bear children. Another seventy thousand people died when the bomb called Fat Man was dropped on Nagasaki. It can be said the entire Japanese population suffered the aftereffects of the bombings of Hiroshima and Nagasaki. Hiroshima was a Japanese trade and military center. Nagasaki was an important port, steel mill, and shipbuilding center.

The use of nuclear weapons was one of the most controversial acts of any president. Today, the decision whether it was wise to drop these bombs is still debated. Historians, political scientists, public affairs commentators, and the public continue to study the decision.

Harry S Truman decided to use nuclear force for several reasons. Japanese cruelty during World War II outraged the world. They had bombed American ships at Pearl Harbor, Hawaii, when they were officially at peace with the United States. After that, Americans were both angry at and afraid of the Japanese who lived in the United States. On February 19, 1942, President Franklin D. Roosevelt signed Executive Order 9066. This order forced almost 120,000 persons of Japanese ancestry into ten internment camps located in the American West. The Japanese left behind homes, possessions, businesses, and farms. Some Japanese from South American countries were also brought to internment camps in the United States. They were not released until the end of the war. Today it is seen as a shameful incident in American history. Most of the Japanese Americans were loyal citizens,

The second atomic bomb was dropped on Nagasaki, Japan, on August 9, 1945.

and many fought with United States troops.

In addition, the Japanese had forced American soldiers on death marches in the Pacific Islands. The most famous was the Bataan Death March in the Philippines. Men were made to march without sufficient rest or food or water. When they dropped behind, they were executed. Americans had little pity for the Japanese.[3] Families of soldiers fighting in the Pacific wanted their loved ones home.

With Britain's Churchill, Truman realized that a prolonged war in the Pacific would be to the disadvantage of Eastern Europe. It would require stationing allied troops in the Pacific when they were severely needed in Europe. The two world leaders also feared that the Soviet Union would invade Manchuria, Korea, and possibly even Japan. The USSR was already in control of much of Eastern Europe, and the United States and Britain did not want the Soviets to be too powerful in Asia. In fact, the USSR did invade Manchuria on August 8, 1945.

▶ A Straightforward Decision

Harry Truman believed that dropping the bombs would save American lives. The best estimates of a land invasion of Japan were that it could cost 750,000 American lives. Truman believed that use of nuclear bombs would dramatically shorten the war and potentially save millions of lives, both Japanese and American.[4]

After the bombs were dropped, the Japanese Cabinet Secretary said the bomb "provided an excuse to surrender." Emperor Hirohito's chief civilian advisor said, "the presence of the atomic bomb made it easier for us, the politicians, to negotiate peace." The Japanese saved face, even while surrendering.[5]

Harry Truman alone had made the decision to use weapons of such dramatic destruction. The decision was typical of Truman's presidency. He was a straightforward, no-nonsense man who thought problems through carefully. He defended his decision to use nuclear power until the end of his life. He never expressed any doubt about his decision. In 1972, when Truman was near death in a Kansas City hospital, former Supreme Court Justice Tom Clark visited him. Physicians told Clark he could stay five minutes. Truman kept him for forty-five minutes, talking about the atomic bomb and defending his decision.[6]

Chapter 2

Childhood and Education, 1884–1919

Harry S Truman was born on May 8, 1884. His middle initial does not stand for anything, because his parents could not decide which of two family members to name him after. There is still a controversy over whether or not a period should follow the initial.

A brother, Vivian, was born in 1886, and his sister, Mary Jane, in 1889. Their father, John Anderson Truman, was a farmer and animal trader. Their mother, Martha Ellen, would remain close to Harry all her life. She was an outspoken woman who once said she knew Harry would amount to something from the time he was nine because he "could plow the straightest row of corn in the country."[1] In 1885, the family moved to a farm near Peculiar, Missouri. They moved again in 1887, to a farm owned by Martha Ellen's family. In 1890, they settled in Independence, Missouri, where Harry was raised.

▶ Early Challenges

Harry was diagnosed with extreme nearsightedness as a very young child. He was fitted with thick glasses and

Harry S Truman as a baby.

warned against playing sports. He was a good student who liked to read and play the piano. All of this set him apart from boys his age, and he was afraid of being called a sissy. Later he joked about the label.

After Harry graduated from high school in 1901, he applied for admission to West Point. He was turned down because of his poor eyesight. When his father lost all his money speculating on grain futures, Harry had to go to work rather than to college. He worked briefly in the mailroom of the *Kansas City Star* newspaper, as a timekeeper for a construction company on the Santa Fe Railroad, and for two banks. In 1905, he volunteered for the National Guard and served until 1911.

In 1906, Truman went back to his grandmother's farm at Clinton, Missouri, because the family needed his help. He worked there for the next eleven years. Although he disliked farming, he tried hard to be an efficient farmer, experimenting with techniques such as crop rotation and soil conservation.

Love and War

Truman had gone to high school with a young woman named Bess Wallace. During his years on the farm, they renewed their acquaintance. Truman began to court her. She refused his first offer of

Harry was fitted with eyeglasses as a young child to help correct his weak vision. Here he is pictured in 1897 at the age of thirteen.

marriage. However, by the time he joined the Army in 1917, they were engaged.

Harry Truman went to Europe to fight in World War I at the age of thirty-three. In April 1918, his unit, the 129th Field Artillery regiment, arrived in France. In July, Captain Truman was assigned command of Battery D— 194 men and 167 horses. When the young captain gained control of those unmanageable soldiers, he knew that he could lead men. Later those men would give him a political base in Missouri. Truman saw combat at the battles of St.-Mihiel, Meuse-Argonne, and Verdun. He learned first-hand about trench warfare, poison gas, and the terrible carnage of war. After the November 11 armistice, he had a

Wedding photo of Harry and Bess Truman, June 28, 1919. - Microsoft Internet Explorer

File   Edit   View   Favorites   Tools   Help

Address http://www.whistlestop.org/archive/photos/images/73-1668.htm   Go   Links

Internet

▲ *Harry and Bess on their wedding day, June 28, 1919.*

long wait to be shipped home. He was impatient to get back to Bess.

Harry and Bess were married on June 28, 1919. They moved in with Bess's mother, Mrs. Margaret "Madge" Wallace. She delayed the marriage because she wanted her daughter to marry a "man of means," not a farmer. Truman had to work hard to prove to her that he was worthy of Bess and could support her. The Trumans lived with Mrs. Wallace—or she with them while in the White House—until her death at the end of his presidency. Harry and Bess's only child, Mary Margaret—called Margaret—was born in 1924.

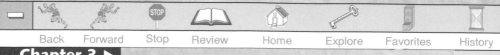
Early Career, 1919–1945

From 1919 until 1922, Truman operated a haberdashery, or men's clothing store, with Eddie Jacobson, an old friend. The business failed during a nationwide recession. Jacobson declared bankruptcy. Truman refused to join his friend in this decision. It took Truman fifteen years to pay off the debts from the store.

The Triangle Club, 1921 This picture was taken in Swope Park, Kansas City, Missouri. Truman is - Micr...

File   Edit   View   Favorites   Tools   Help

Address http://www.whistlestop.org/archive/photos/images/62-145.htm   Go   Links

Internet

▲ Truman ran a men's clothing store from 1919 until 1922. He is pictured here with the Triangle Club in 1921, an association of merchants.

▶ Entering Politics

Truman next turned to politics. Michael J. Pendergast was the political boss for the eastern part of Jackson County. He was the older brother of Tom Pendergast, the political boss who controlled Kansas City. At that time, many cities were controlled by "bosses." They put up candidates, got out the vote, and controlled the business side of running the city. Mike Pendergast proposed Truman for county judge—an administrative position. Harry Truman, however, ran as an independent rather than with Pendergast's backing. He announced his candidacy at a meeting of veterans. Pendergast backed him once he began to campaign because he seemed to be a winning candidate. Both the Pendergasts and Truman were loyal Democratic Party members.

Elected to the three-member board of judges, Truman began a reform campaign. He served from January 1, 1923, until January 1, 1925, but lost the election because both the Ku Klux Klan and the National Association for the Advancement of Colored People (NAACP) opposed him. The Klan had grown in membership since Truman's 1923 election. Its members remembered that he had refused to pledge not to appoint Catholics to county jobs. The NAACP opposed him because he had exposed a rival politician's plan to build and name after himself an outrageously expensive and elaborate home for African-American boys. Truman was elected as a presiding judge in 1927 and served until 1935.[1]

Previously the courts had granted building contracts to local contractors, often overlooking poor quality materials and workmanship. Truman gave the contracts to the lowest bidder. Local contractors protested to Tom Pendergast. Truman refused to change his decisions. When

tax evasion. Most of the one million dollars he owed in taxes had been spent gambling on horses. Truman, a truly honest man, was shocked by the news.

The Truman Committee

In 1940, Truman announced that he would run again for the Senate even if the only vote he got would be his own. Roosevelt offered him a seat on the Interstate Commerce Commission if he would withdraw from the race. Despite the promise of better pay and lifetime security, Truman refused. No one thought Truman had a chance. Then in April, Roosevelt withdrew his backing from Truman's opponent and old enemy, former Missouri Governor Lloyd Stark, and gave it to Truman. Again Truman campaigned tirelessly in the middle of a scorching summer. He won both the primary and the election.

Back in the Senate, the increasing signs of war alarmed Truman. He suspected there was dishonesty and waste in government contracts. He toured the country inspecting the defense program. He also served as chairman of the Truman Committee, a five-senator watchdog committee that investigated defense spending. This group discovered many violations of the defense program. For example, Alcoa Aluminum had control of the aluminum market and could set prices as high as it wished, and the government would have to pay them. He also found that the country faced a serious rubber shortage and that defective engines were being used in military equipment.

An Abrupt Vice Presidency

The Japanese attacked Pearl Harbor on December 7, 1941, forcing the United States to declare war. Truman volunteered for active duty but was refused because of his

Tools   Search   Notes   Discuss   Go!

age. He was also told his presence in the Senate was more valuable to the country. Because of his committee work, Senator Truman's prestige grew. In addition, he possessed the ability to get along with all factions of his party.

For the 1944 presidential race, Roosevelt wanted a new vice presidential candidate. Vice President Henry Wallace was no longer popular among the party leadership. Some considered him a radical. Roosevelt called on Truman to run. Truman accepted only after he was persuaded that his refusal would tear the Democratic Party in half. At the Democratic convention, it first seemed a close call between sitting Vice President Wallace and Truman. Then states began to swing their votes, and Truman won the nomination. There was no doubt that Roosevelt, always extremely popular with the American people, would win

▲ President Franklin D. Roosevelt (right) with his vice president, Harry S Truman.

the election. After the inauguration, Truman was vice president to a man he hardly knew. Roosevelt made little effort to involve Truman in executive decisions or acquaint him with foreign affairs.

Franklin Delano Roosevelt's health had been failing for years due to the cumulative effects of polio. Still, his death on April 12, 1945, was sudden and unexpected. Truman was sworn in as the thirty-third president of the United States the same day. Victory in Europe was declared in May 1945, less than one month after he had taken the oath of office.

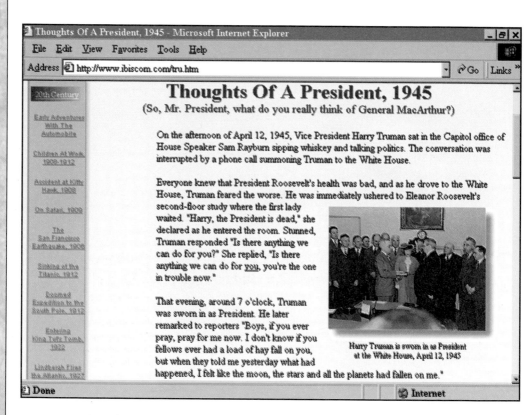

Thoughts Of A President, 1945
(So, Mr. President, what do you really think of General MacArthur?)

On the afternoon of April 12, 1945, Vice President Harry Truman sat in the Capitol office of House Speaker Sam Rayburn sipping whiskey and talking politics. The conversation was interrupted by a phone call summoning Truman to the White House.

Everyone knew that President Roosevelt's health was bad, and as he drove to the White House, Truman feared the worse. He was immediately ushered to Eleanor Roosevelt's second-floor study where the first lady waited. "Harry, the President is dead," she declared as he entered the room. Stunned, Truman responded "Is there anything we can do for you?" She replied, "Is there anything we can do for you, you're the one in trouble now."

That evening, around 7 o'clock, Truman was sworn in as President. He later remarked to reporters "Boys, if you ever pray, pray for me now. I don't know if you fellows ever had a load of hay fall on you, but when they told me yesterday what had happened, I felt like the moon, the stars and all the planets had fallen on me."

Harry Truman is sworn in as President at the White House, April 12, 1945

When President Roosevelt died suddenly on April 12, 1945, a startled Truman assumed the role as president. The next day he stated, "I felt like the moon, the stars and all the planets had fallen on me."

First Term, 1945–1948

As president, Truman was very successful in foreign affairs. He made the United States an active participant in the affairs of the world, rather than an observer. Roosevelt had believed that the United States could win victories in Europe and Japan and the other islands of the Pacific and then withdraw from world politics. Truman understood that this was not possible.

▶ Major Foreign Policy Accomplishments

Before Roosevelt's death, plans were underway for the establishment of an international peace group, later to be known as the United Nations (UN), and for the unconditional surrender of Germany. Truman's skill as a statesman assured the fulfillment of both these plans. He flew to San Francisco to sign the charter for the United Nations in April. Germany surrendered unconditionally on May 8, 1945.

In July, the new president went to the Potsdam Conference in northeast Germany. Truman liked and respected both Winston Churchill of England and Joseph Stalin of the Soviet Union. He would soon learn that he could not trust Stalin. Truman and Churchill became colleagues. They thought alike and supported each other on questions of international policy. Churchill became a frequent visitor to the Truman White House.

The conference led to some decisions regarding Germany. The Big Three decided that Germany would no longer be allowed to have its own military. The German

Back   Forward   Stop   Review   Home   Explore   Favorites   History

Premier Joseph Stalin, President Truman, and Prime Minister Winston Churchill, July 17, 1945. - Microso...

File   Edit   View   Favorites   Tools   Help

Address http://www.whistlestop.org/archive/photos/images/62-770.htm

Done   Internet

▲ *Premier Joseph Stalin, President Truman, and Prime Minister Winston Churchill, attended the Potsdam Conference in July 1945.*

industries that produced military supplies were dismantled as well. The Nazi Party was dissolved and its laws and government institutions were disbanded. Finally, Germany had to agree to pay reparations, or fines, to the countries and peoples it had attacked during the war.

The Truman Doctrine and the Marshall Plan were major foreign policy accomplishments of Truman's first term of office. The Truman Doctrine promised assistance to nations resisting Communist aggression from within, or from outside forces. Turkey and Greece were granted such aid. It set the standard by which the United States committed itself to preventing the spread of Communism throughout the world.

The Marshall Plan provided funds to aid Europe in recovery from the destruction of World War II. Truman knew that European governments weakened by the war could collapse and be easy targets of Communist takeover without economic aid. Truman's point was clearly made when Communists in Czechoslovakia caused non-Communists to resign from their posts in the government, and then created a Communist government in February 1948.

Domestic Policies

Truman was not as successful in his proposals for change at home. To avoid a postwar depression in the country, he sent a twenty-one-point message to Congress. It contained such measures as right-to-work laws, veterans' programs, aid to small businesses, a housing program, and an anti-discrimination bill. He called his program the Fair Deal. It did not get the support of Congress.

During Truman's first presidency, both railroad workers and coal miners went on strike, severely crippling the day-to-day operation of the country. Yet, Truman vetoed the Taft-Hartley Bill outlawing strikes by entire industries. He thought it unfairly punished labor unions. Congress overrode his veto, but after that Truman always had the support of the labor unions.

A Crash in the White House

One night in 1947, Truman noticed the chandelier above him was swaying. It was during an official reception at the White House. Later, Margaret Truman's piano fell through the floor of her sitting room. Investigation

Truman Announced A Fair Deal - Microsoft Internet Explorer

File   Edit   View   Favorites   Tools   Help

Address   http://www.americaslibrary.gov/pages/jb_0105_fairdeal_2.html   Go   Links

★Home   ★About this site   ★Help   The Library of Congress

America's Story
from America's Library

Meet Amazing Americans   **Jump Back in Time**   Explore the States   Join America at Play   See, Hear and Sing

Jump Back in Time ▶ Modern Era (1946 - present)

PRESIDENT TRUMAN WIPES OUT SEGREGATION IN ARMED FORCES

Posse, Bent On Lynching, Searches Woods For Prey

Truman Announced A Fair Deal
January 5, 1949
Truman's plans were not popular with the members of Congress. They rejected his plans for national health insurance though they did raise the minimum wage. What about equal employment rights for all Americans?

◀ BACK   page 2 of 3   NEXT ▶

Truman's executive order wipes out segregation in armed forces, July 31, 1948

Click for enlargement and credits

Internet

▲ On July 26, 1948, Truman signed an executive order, which demanded desegregation of the armed forces. His actions marked the beginning of a long struggle to end prejudice in the United States.

revealed that the White House was structurally unsound. It was not safe for occupancy. The Trumans moved across the street to the Blair House while the White House was rebuilt. It was difficult for Truman to conduct both the day-to-day affairs of the presidency and official entertaining from these smaller quarters.[1]

▶ Capturing the Vote

Early in 1948, Truman sent Congress a strong message calling for measures to end racial discrimination. Racial prejudice was still strong in the country at the time.

Truman himself was a product of southern culture, where prejudice was still common. Still, he was outraged at the violence against African Americans in the South, especially against returning soldiers. On July 26, 1948, Truman signed Executive Order 9981 ordering desegregation of the armed forces. Although desegregation was not complete for many years, this was an important beginning. Angry southerners in Congress accused Truman of trying to capture the vote of African Americans in the North in the forthcoming election.

Similarly, Truman was accused of trying to capture the Jewish vote. He backed the idea of a homeland in Palestine for Jews displaced by World War II and the Holocaust. Pentagon officials worried that by backing Jewish rights, Truman was alienating Arab nations and jeopardizing the major source of oil for the nation. If war with the Soviet

▲ *President Truman making a campaign speech in Washington, D.C.*

Union came, as was always a possibility, Arab oil would be badly needed.

A Run for the Presidency

Truman was not seeking votes in these actions. Actually he had not decided whether to run. Once, he mentioned the possibility of running on the Democratic ticket with General Dwight D. Eisenhower and offered to run as his vice president. Eisenhower, or "Ike," as he was known, turned him down. Truman knew that Bess desperately wanted to leave the White House. Then, too, he found no satisfaction in being president. Still, he seemed to enjoy the challenge, and he probably wanted to be elected in his own right.[2]

When Truman announced his candidacy for president, the sons of former President Roosevelt started a move to draft Eisenhower for the Democratic Party nomination. Again, Ike refused. (It would later be apparent he was a Republican.) Henry Wallace, once fired by Truman as secretary of commerce, traveled the country, gathering crowds to whom he preached a liberal agenda. This included turning atomic arms over to the United Nations and the United States' financing of reconstruction of the Soviet Union. Reluctantly, the Democratic Party nominated Truman, who promised them a victory. Southerners bolted the party and became the Dixiecrats, under the leadership of Strom Thurmond of South Carolina. Wallace's followers formed Progressive Citizens of America and nominated Wallace. The Republicans nominated Thomas Dewey.

"Dewey Defeats Truman"

Always known for salty language, Truman told his vice presidential running mate, Alben Barkley, "I'm going to

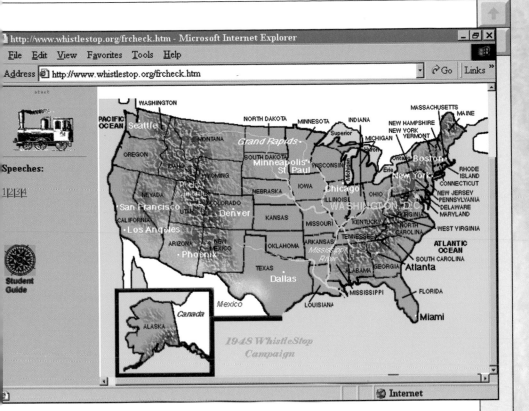

This interactive map shows the states Truman visited on his 1948 Whistlestop campaign. During his campaign, Truman traveled more than 31,000 miles and delivered over 350 speeches.

give 'em hell!"[3] But almost no one believed that he would win, especially with Wallace and Thurmond splitting the party vote.

Truman campaigned at his usual tireless pace. He spoke in thousands of small towns and big cities from the open platform of his special railroad car. Patriotism, love of the land, and the values of small-town America were regular topics. As the election drew near, almost every poll predicted that Dewey would be the next president.

On election night, Truman enjoyed a brief, early lead. Then, Dewey carried New York, which meant Truman

http://www.trumanlibrary.org/photos/s8-777.gif - Microsoft Internet Explorer

File   Edit   View   Favorites   Tools   Help

Address http://www.trumanlibrary.org/photos/s8-777.gif   Go   Links

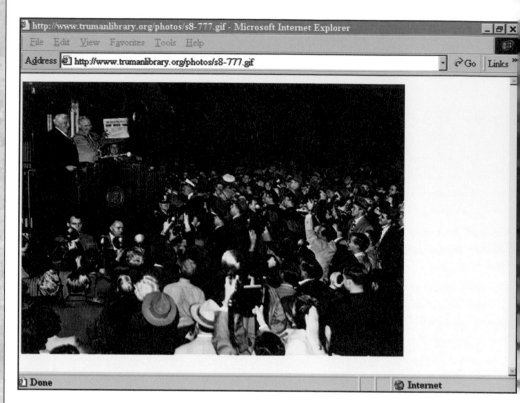

Done   Internet

▲ *Because many voters thought Dewey had won the election, fewer than half of the eligible citizens went to the voting booths. In this famous photograph, Truman smiles as he holds up the* Chicago Tribune, *which printed "Dewey Defeats Truman" as its front-page headline.*

would have to carry several major Midwestern states. Truman went to bed, only to be awakened at four o'clock in the morning by his aides who told him he had the lead. The next morning, a triumphant Truman waved a copy of the *Chicago Tribune* at reporters. The mistaken headline read, "Dewey Defeats Truman." Fewer than half the eligible citizens voted in the election.[4] Anticipating that Dewey would win, many voters who could have voted for him and secured his victory stayed home. Truman's victory was probably the biggest upset in political history and one of the greatest personal victories of any American politician.[5]

Second Term, 1949–1953

When he was inaugurated in 1949, Truman announced his Point Four Program for foreign policy. He called for support of the United Nations, support of the Marshall Plan, military assistance to stop Communist aggression, and the sharing of scientific and industrial progress with undeveloped parts of the world.

A Second Honeymoon

For the first six months of his second term, Truman seemed to be enjoying a second honeymoon with the American people. He had a Democratic majority in Congress. On April 4, 1949, the United States, Canada, and ten Western European nations signed the North Atlantic Treaty, a peacetime military alliance against the Soviet Union. Together, these nations became known as NATO. By then the Soviet Union had exploded its own atomic bomb, and soon formed its own alliance called The Warsaw Pact.

The Red Scare

Trouble came later that year. For some time, Congress had been investigating Communist infiltration in the administrations of both Roosevelt and Truman. A confessed former Communist, Whittaker Chambers, implicated Alger Hiss. Hiss, at that time, was president of the Carnegie Foundation for International Peace. In spite of Hiss's protests of innocence, Congressman Richard Nixon of

California pursued a highly publicized investigation. After two trials, Hiss eventually was found guilty of perjury.

Klaus Fuchs, a British scientist who had worked at the nuclear facility in Los Alamos, New Mexico, confessed early in 1950 to having given atomic secrets to the Soviet Union. Four days later, Truman reacted by announcing plans to intensify efforts to develop the deadly hydrogen bomb. Fuchs's confession probably gave Senator Joseph McCarthy of Wisconsin his ticket to fame. McCarthy announced that he had a lengthy list of alleged Communists working for the government. Although his charges were unsupported, the movement known as McCarthyism, or the Red Scare, grew. McCarthy's Senate committee targeted politicians, artists, actors, and intellectuals. Many careers were ruined before McCarthy was exposed as an extremist and a liar. Truman despised McCarthy and made it no secret in his correspondence to the senator.

▶ Communist Invasion in China

Meanwhile the news from China was discouraging. Communists were overrunning Chiang Kai-shek, whose government the United States supported. Among the American people there was talk of the "Red Tide" in Asia that could threaten half the world.[1] Chiang Kai-shek eventually withdrew to the island of Taiwan off the coast of mainland China, with United States' support, and China became a vast Communist country. North Korea was part of the Chinese Communist movement though it maintained a separate government. Truman was accused of "losing China."[2] Some felt that his administration had not done enough to stop the Communists, led by Mao Tse-tung, from taking over the country.

The Korean War

In June 1950, North Korean soldiers crossed the 38th parallel into South Korea. Truman had signed a defense policy with South Korea and had refused to deal with Kim Il Sung, Communist dictator of North Korea. Truman ordered the evacuation of American dependents from South Korea and authorized the bombing of airfields and military targets in North Korea. He also called on the United Nations to defend South Korea, which it did. Truman called this a "police action" and expected a quick resolution to the situation. Truman met with U.N.

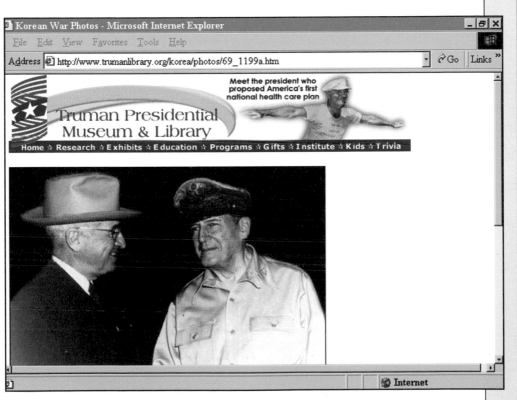

President Truman and General Douglas MacArthur met for the first time on Wake Island, October 14, 1950. Less than two months later, Truman fired MacArthur for ruining the peace talks Truman had been trying to negotiate with China.

Commander General Douglas MacArthur at Wake Island, and the general assured him of a quick victory. He did not want to send ground troops although he eventually did. Many feared this "police action" would signal the beginning of a third world war.

MacArthur was in charge of American troops in the Pacific. On November 28, 1950, the Communist Chinese struck United Nations forces in large numbers, causing one of the greatest crises of Truman's presidency.[3] MacArthur wanted to bomb supply routes in Manchuria with nuclear weapons, to which Truman agreed, but Truman wanted to avoid war with China. He ordered a retreat, which became a defeat.

In December 1950, the war was going badly. Truman was worried. The Chinese had entered the conflict on the side of North Korea. They had threatened to do so if United Nations troops crossed the 38th parallel. United Nations troops were now in a massive retreat south. General Oliver P. Smith and his Marines were surrounded by overwhelming Chinese troops at Chosin Reservoir, north of the 38th parallel. In an amazing campaign of thirteen days, the Marines fought their way eighty miles to the sea and supported naval forces. They often fought hand-to-hand in blinding blizzards. Being

◀ *Truman declared a national emergency against North Korea on December 16, 1950.*

forced from North Korea was a major defeat for United Nations troops, but the Battle of Chosin momentarily paralyzed the fighting. Estimates are that the Chinese lost twenty-five thousand men, while the Marines lost only about seven hundred. The fighting began to seesaw back and forth, with neither army winning a clear battle. The city of Seoul, South Korea, changed hands four times during the war. This indicates how indecisive the fighting was.

MacArthur loudly criticized the United States' policy, in spite of Truman's orders to stop making public statements. Finally, MacArthur issued his own ultimatum to China, thereby ruining the peace talks that Truman had been trying to negotiate. Truman asked for MacArthur's resignation, but the general refused to return to the States. When Truman finally fired him in April 1951, there was a public outcry because MacArthur was a national hero. Some called for Truman's impeachment. However, firing MacArthur has often been called one of Truman's most correct and courageous decisions.[4]

Truman was beset by other troubles. One of his lifetime friends and press secretary, Charlie Ross, died suddenly. A day or two later, Margaret Truman, a professional soprano, gave the final concert of her tour. She knew that it was not one of her best performances and attributed it to Ross's death and the ongoing conflict in Korea. Paul Hume, critic for the *Washington Post,* wrote a negative review of the concert. Truman, already emotionally strained, wrote an angry letter to Hume that became public. Margaret was embarrassed, Hume was gracious, and Truman refused to apologize. The story has become a classic one about Truman's stubbornness.

▶ Problems in the Administration

By the last year of Truman's second term, the fighting in Korea had lasted almost as long as World War I. United Nations forces sometimes gained ground, but often they lost to overwhelming numbers of soldiers from China. Truman refused to sign a treaty that would return refugees to North Korea against their will. He knew they would be killed. The war overshadowed Truman's second term. Yet, he believed holding the line against aggression by Communist China was important for the future of the free world.

Meanwhile, at home, the administration was under attack. The Fulbright Committee investigated financial misconduct involving government loans to small businesses. The Kefauver Committee investigated criminal activity, with implications that some officials within the federal government were aiding criminals. Also, there was close scrutiny of the way income taxes were assessed and collected. Perhaps the final straw was a scandal at the West Point Military Academy in which great numbers of students were dismissed for cheating on examinations.

▶ An End to the Presidency

A high point for Truman came when his family moved back into the newly renovated and restored White House. Truman took television reporters on a tour and even

◀ *Bess Truman (left) and Mamie Eisenhower.*

played Mozart's Ninth Sonata on the Steinway piano in the East Room to demonstrate the tone and acoustics.

Truman was ready to leave the presidency. He had once said, "Any man in his right mind would never want to be president."[5] The problem was to find the right man to run on the Democratic ticket for the 1952 presidential election. Truman decided on Governor Adlai Stevenson of Illinois. When Stevenson initially declined, Truman thought about running again. Truman's closest advisors cautioned him against it. Stevenson finally agreed to run.

General Dwight David Eisenhower won the election. Truman had campaigned hard for Stevenson even though he knew Stevenson was a reluctant candidate. In addition, Stevenson was in the uncomfortable position of running against a war hero. Truman was, as always, fiercely loyal to the Democratic Party. His relations with Eisenhower, who he had once admired, had become strained and difficult.

Although it happened after he was out of office, Truman must be given much of the credit for the armistice that finally ended the Korean War. Signed on July 27, 1953, it established a demilitarized zone as the border between North and South Korea.

Chapter 6

Retirement and Legacy, 1953–1972

Truman and his family were relieved to leave the White House because they were tired of the public spotlight. Although Bess Truman had been a capable first lady, she was more inclined to be a private person. As a young single woman, Margaret Truman resented the constant attention to her every move. Truman also welcomed his new independence from Secret Service protection, but some said he found the readjustment to private life difficult.[1]

▶ Retirement

After his retirement, Truman took a daily walk, kept up with correspondence, wrote his memoirs, lectured at

▲ Bess Truman, Eleanor Roosevelt, Earl Warren, Herbert Hoover, Basil O'Connor, and Harry Truman at the dedication of the Truman Library, July 6, 1957.

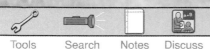
universities, and made speeches for the Democrats. He campaigned for Stevenson's second try at the presidency in 1956 and, with better results, for John F. Kennedy in 1960. He supervised the building of the Truman Library in his hometown of Independence, Missouri. The library was dedicated in 1957.

His beloved daughter, Margaret, married journalist Clifton Daniel, Jr., and had four sons. Truman was a devoted grandfather, although not the kind to roughhouse with the boys. Margaret became a well-known mystery writer and the author of one of the best biographies written about her father.

After suffering from health problems for several years, Truman died at the age of eighty-eight in 1972. His wife, Bess, lived to be ninety-seven.

Truman's Legacy

When Truman left office, he was not regarded as a great or even good president. People took him at his word that he was an average, ordinary man who just happened to be president. He only began to be appreciated in the 1970s. Still controversial, he is now regarded as one of the near-great presidents of the twentieth century because of his accomplishments in foreign affairs. He was less successful in getting his domestic programs—dealing with civil rights, and the Fair Deal—through the legislature.

Today, Truman is considered a man of great honesty and integrity, who did his duty without personal gain. He made difficult decisions, such as dropping the atomic bomb, supporting South Korea, and firing General MacArthur, without questioning his own judgment.

He sometimes made quick decisions, and he was touchy about both his own reputation and that of his

family. Praised for his blunt, plain manner of speaking, he made no secret of his dislikes, including people. Clearly, he was a man who grew into the job given him—and did it with great courage and skill.

Truman himself once wrote, "Our greatest presidents and congressional leaders have been the ones who have been vilified the worst."[2]

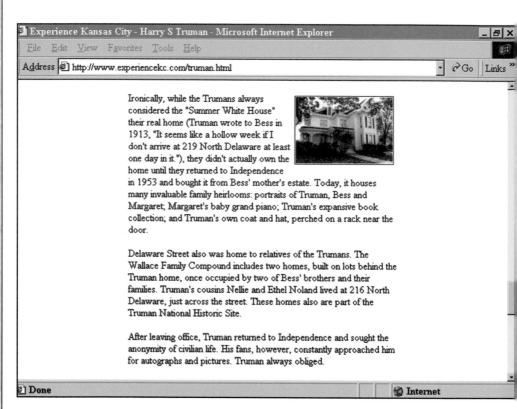

The Trumans' "Summer White House" is now home to a collection of various family heirlooms, such as Margaret's baby grand piano, as well as Truman's book collection, coat, and hat.

Chapter Notes

Chapter 1. The Atomic Bomb, August 1945

1. David McCullough, *Truman* (New York: Simon & Schuster, 1992), p. 424.

2. Margaret Truman, *Harry S. Truman* (New York: William Morrow & Company, Inc., 1973), p. 279.

3. Robert H. Ferrell, *Harry S. Truman: A Life* (Columbia: University of Missouri Press, 1994), p. 210.

4. Ibid., p. 273.

5. Ibid., p. 284.

6. Robert H. Ferrell, "Harry S. Truman: A 50th Anniversary Commemoration of his *Presidency,*" *Secretary of State—State of Missouri*, July 1996, <http://mos/sos.state.mo.us/ofman/truman.html> (September 13, 2001).

Chapter 2. Childhood and Education, 1884–1919

1. Robert H. Ferrell, *Harry S. Truman: A Life* (Columbia: University of Missouri Press, 1994), p. 172.

Chapter 3. Early Career, 1919–1945

1. Robert H. Ferrell, *Harry S. Truman: A Life* (Columbia: University of Missouri Press, 1994), pp. 96–102.

Chapter 4. First Term, 1945–1948

1. Margaret Truman, *Harry S. Truman* (New York: William Morrow & Company, Inc., 1973), pp. 397–398.

2. David McCullough, *Truman* (New York: Simon & Schuster, 1992), pp. 584–585.

3. Paul Boller, *Presidential Anecdotes* (New York: Oxford University Press, 1988), p. 282.

4. Robert H. Ferrell, *Harry S. Truman: A Life* (Columbia: University of Missouri Press, 1994), p. 178.

5. McCullough, p. 709.

Chapter 5. Second Term, 1949–1953

1. David McCullough, *Truman* (New York: Simon & Schuster, 1992), p. 743.

2. Margaret Truman, *Harry S. Truman* (New York: William Morrow & Company, Inc. 1973), p. 410.

3. Ibid., p. 492.

4. McCullough, picture caption no. 18.

5. Truman, p. 36.

Chapter 6. Retirement and Legacy, 1953–1972

1. David McCullough, *Truman* (New York: Simon & Schuster, 1992), p. 932.

2. Robert H. Ferrell, *Harry S. Truman: A Life* (Columbia: University of Missouri Press, 1994), p. 183.

Further Reading

Fleming, Thomas. *Harry S Truman.* New York: Walker and Company, 1993.

Ferrell, Robert H. *Harry S. Truman: A Life.* Columbia: University of Missouri Press, 1996.

Hargrove, Jim. *Harry S. Truman.* Chicago: Children's Press, 1987.

Joseph, Paul. *Harry Truman.* Edina, Minn.: ABDO Publishing Company, 1999.

Lindop, Edmund. *Woodrow Wilson, Franklin D. Roosevelt, Harry S. Truman.* Brookfield, Conn.: Twenty-first Century Books, Inc., 1995.

McCullough, David. *Truman.* New York: Simon & Schuster, 1992.

Sandak, Cass R. *The Trumans.* New York: Crestwood House, 1992.

Schuman, Michael A. *Harry S. Truman.* Berkeley Heights, N.J.: Enslow Publishers, 1997.

Truman, Margaret. *Harry S. Truman.* New York: Morrow Avon, 1993.

Index